Mission to Madagascar

Adventures of Riley

Mission to Madagascar

Dear Riley,

Will you join me, Aunt Martha, and Cousin Alice on a mission to the African island of Madagascar?

We will be working with a film crew to study lemurs and other **endemic** wildlife species (animals found nowhere else in the world!). Our goal is to find the rare and mysterious aye-aye lemur. By capturing one on film, we hope to show people everywhere why it is so important to preserve Madagascar's unique habitats and animals.

Finding an aye-aye will be tricky since they live alone and only come out at night. I hope your answer is **aye-aye!** :)

Uncle Max

BY **Amanda Lumry** AND **Laura Hurwitz**

ILLUSTRATIONS BY **Sarah McIntyre**

SCHOLASTIC INC.

New York • Toronto • London • Auckland • Sydney
Mexico City • New Delhi • Hong Kong • Buenos Aires

A special thank-you to all the scientists who collaborated on this project. Your time and assistance are very much appreciated. Additional thanks to Royal Botanic Gardens, Kew, for use of its library and for its research material on Madagascar vegetation.

First published in China in 2005 by Eaglemont Press.
www.eaglemont.com

Image credits:
Cover road with baobab trees, page 13 rain forest, pages 14–15 rain forest, pages 18–19 rain forest, pages 20–21 rain forest © Altrendo Nature/Getty Images
Title page ruffed lemur © Anup Shah/Getty Images
Pages 4–5 baobab trees lining road © Raphael Van Butsele/Getty Images
Page 10 black and white ruffed lemur, page 12 leaf-tailed gecko © Kevin Schafer/Getty Images
Page 16 indri lemur in tree © John Giustina/Getty Images
Page 17 Madagascar tree boa © Gerry Ellis/Getty Images
Page 17 diademed sifaka © Pete Oxford/Getty Images
Page 19 giraffe weevil © Frank Greenaway/Getty Images
Page 19 Parson's chameleon © Art Wolfe/Getty Images
Page 20 fossa © Roy Toft/Getty Images
Page 29 aye-aye © James Martin/Getty Images

Illustrations © 2005 by Sarah McIntyre
Additional Illustrations and Layouts by Ulkatay and Ulkatay, London WC2E 9RZ
Editing and Digital Compositing by Michael E. Penman

Library of Congress Control Number: 2005001350

ISBN-13: 978-0-545-06857-4
ISBN-10: 0-545-06857-6

10 9 8 7 6 5 4 3 2 1   09 10 11 12 13

Printed in the U.S.A.   08
First Scholastic paperback printing, February 2009

FSC

Mixed Sources
Product group from well-managed forests, controlled sources and recycled wood or fiber
Cert no. SGS-COC-003338
www.fsc.org
© 1996 Forest Stewardship Council

A portion of the proceeds from your purchase of this licensed product supports the stated educational mission of the Smithsonian Institution— "the increase and diffusion of knowledge." The name of the Smithsonian Institution and the sunburst logo are registered trademarks of the Smithsonian Institution and are registered in the U.S. Patent and Trademark Office. www.si.edu

2% of the proceeds from this book will be donated to the Wildlife Conservation Society. http://wcs.org

We try to produce the most beautiful books possible and we are extremely concerned about the impact of our manufacturing process on the forests of the world and the environment as a whole. Accordingly, we made sure that the paper used in this book has been certified as coming from forests that are managed to insure the protection of the people and wildlife dependent upon them.

"I can't believe I'm going to Madagascar to look for lemurs," said Riley.

"Elephants and lions, too?" asked Mike.

"Probably, but we're mainly looking for a rare lemur called the aye-aye. It only comes out at night," said Riley. The thought gave him the shivers.

Uncle Max and Aunt Martha greeted Riley at the London airport.

"Is that Alice?" Riley asked.

"She thinks this is her chance to be a movie star," chuckled Uncle Max.

Alice glided over. "Hello, darling! Do you like my new look?"

2

From London they flew to Antananarivo, the capital of Madagascar.

"Now we have to pick up the film crew in the Spiny Forest," said Uncle Max. "Then we'll drive to our lodge in the East Central Rain Forest."

"How about some tasty **kitoza** and rice porridge for breakfast?" asked Aunt Martha.

"I would love some," said Max.

"I'm too sleepy to eat." Alice yawned.

"So am I," said Riley.

3

Baobab Tree

➤ This tree looks like it is growing upside down, with its roots in the air!

➤ It can live for several thousand years.

➤ Bats and lemurs **pollinate** the tree.

➤ Sometimes its trunk is wide enough to be used as a house.

—Laurence J. Dorr,
Associate Curator, Botany,
National Museum of Natural History,
Smithsonian Institution

4

"Are those things really trees?" asked Riley.

"They sure are," said Aunt Martha. "They're called baobabs, and they survive the dry desert climate by storing water in their trunks."

"There's the film crew!" Alice squealed.

She tossed her feather boa over her shoulder and dashed out to meet them.

"I'm Brigitte and this is my husband, Carlos," the woman said. "We're almost packed and ready to go."

"It's going to be hard to leave these beautiful trees behind," said Carlos.

"They are pretty amazing," gushed Alice. "Just point the camera at me and I'll tell you all about them!"

"Oops! I think we just ran out of film," said Brigitte.

At the lodge, they were met by a local man named Jaona.

"When does the filming begin?" asked Alice. Before anyone could answer, Aunt Martha lifted a huge insect out of Alice's hair. Alice screamed.

"It's just a hissing cockroach," said Aunt Martha. "They make great pets."

"That's true!" said Jaona. "Your rooms are this way. I'm sure you're all tired after such a long drive."

Hissing Cockroach

➤ The male has large "horns" that it uses to fight with other males.

➤ This cockroach doesn't have any wings.

➤ When disturbed, it makes a loud hissing sound.

—Norbert Andrianarivelo,
Research Scientist,
Wildlife Conservation Society

Nighttime came quickly.

Riley lay awake, thinking about the strange aye-aye living somewhere in the dark forest.

Tap . . . tap . . . scratch . . . scratch.

What was that?

Was he dreaming?

He peeked through the curtain. Two odd lights glowed from the tree branches. Heart pounding, Riley pulled the blanket over his head, hoping it would protect him through the night.

"Let's go!" cried Alice. "The film crew is waiting!" Morning had come, but Uncle Max and Aunt Martha were having a hard time getting out of bed.

"I feel awful," Uncle Max groaned.

"Me, too," said Aunt Martha. "Maybe we shouldn't have eaten that **kitoza**."

"Alice, you and Riley will have to go without us," said Uncle Max.

"No problem!" said Alice.

Painted Mantella Frog

► The male makes very loud call sounds.

► The female can lay up to 27 eggs at once.

► Yellow, green, and black coloring usually means that it's poisonous. Don't touch!

—Don E. Wilson, Senior Scientist, Smithsonian Institution

The first thing they saw were black and white ruffed lemurs leaping from branch to branch.

"Most lemurs are arboreal. That means they live in trees," said Brigitte.

"Aye-ayes are arboreal and **nocturnal**, so we probably won't see any until after dark," said Alice, leaning against a tree.

"Brigitte, zoom in by Alice!" said Carlos. Alice struck a pose. This was her big chance!

Black and White Ruffed Lemur

➤ Rain is no problem for this lemur. It has long, waterproof fur.

➤ It is found very high up in tall trees in the rain forest.

➤ It is the only lemur that makes a fur-lined nest.

—Vanessa Rasoamampianina,
Research Scientist,
Wildlife Conservation Society

"Wonderful!" said Carlos.

Alice smiled.

"I almost didn't see that leaf-tailed gecko," said Brigitte.

"The what?" asked Alice. They weren't filming her at all.

Leaf-Tailed Gecko

➤ This gecko has a flat tail and body.

➤ During the day, its **iris** becomes a very small vertical line to help keep sunlight out.

➤ The edges of its skin lie flat against the tree, making it difficult for predators to see.

—Achille Raselimanana, Biodiversity Programme Officer, World Wildlife Fund Madagascar & West Indian Ocean Programme Office

12

That night, Uncle Max and Aunt Martha still felt sick, so Riley and Alice grabbed their **headlamps** and once again joined Carlos and Brigitte.

"Where are you going?" asked Jaona.

"To look for aye-ayes," said Alice.

"Many local people believe aye-ayes are a sign of bad luck, so they kill them on sight," said Jaona.

"That's too bad," said Brigitte. "We hope our work will show that aye-ayes are important to Madagascar, and that not seeing them would be far more unlucky than seeing them."

In the dark, the forest seemed to close in around them. Riley and Alice stuck to Carlos like glue.

They didn't spot
any aye-ayes, and
Riley was glad.

19

The next morning, Uncle Max and Aunt Martha woke the children.

"Hear those indris?" Uncle Max boomed. "Time to get up! That's your Madagascar alarm clock!"

Uncle Max made up for lost time by opening up the forest to them.

Rufous-Headed Ground-Roller

➤ It hides in the deep shade, making it hard to spot.

➤ It loves to sing and can often be heard on forest walks.

➤ It builds its nest on the ground.

—Dr. George Powell, Senior Conservation Scientist, and Suzanne Palminteri, Senior Conservation Specialist, World Wildlife Fund

Indri

➤ It sings one song each day to communicate its **territory**. The song lasts from 1 to 4 minutes.

➤ The Malagasy named it *babakoto*, which means "father of a little boy." That is because its call sounds like a father searching for his missing son.

—Aleta Quinn, Research Collaborator, Smithsonian Institution

Madagascar Tree Boa

➤ It hunts for small animals or birds using a heat-sensitive gland on its snout.

➤ When a female is pregnant, her skin will darken to help absorb more sunlight for warmth.

—Herilala Randrimahazo, Research Scientist, Wildlife Conservation Society

Diademed Sifaka

➤ Its hind legs are strong and long, so it can jump from tree to tree.

➤ Its only predators are humans and the fossa.

—Dr. Sheila M. O'Connor, Conservation Measures and Audits, World Wildlife Fund International

Blue Coua

➤ It is related to the cuckoo and is only found in Madagascar.

➤ It gets its name from the color of the skin around its eyes.

➤ A female lays only one egg at a time.

—Dr. Nancy J. Clum, Assistant Curator, Ornithology, Wildlife Conservation Society

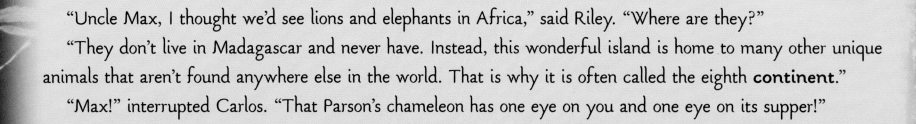

"Uncle Max, I thought we'd see lions and elephants in Africa," said Riley. "Where are they?"

"They don't live in Madagascar and never have. Instead, this wonderful island is home to many other unique animals that aren't found anywhere else in the world. That is why it is often called the eighth **continent**."

"Max!" interrupted Carlos. "That Parson's chameleon has one eye on you and one eye on its supper!"

Giraffe Weevil

➤ It is an insect from the beetle family.

➤ There are 60,000 different kinds of weevils, making it the largest animal family in the world!

➤ It is 3 in. (7.6 cm) long.

➤ Its eggs are laid in wood. Once hatched, the young tunnel and feed.

—Gary Hevel,
Public Information Officer,
Smithsonian Institution

Suddenly, the chameleon's tongue darted out and snapped up a nearby giraffe weevil.

"Yuck," said Alice.

"Did you know that chameleons communicate by changing color?" asked Uncle Max. "Green means calm and yellow means angry."

Parson's Chameleon

➤ Some local people believe it is poisonous to the touch, but this is not true.

➤ It can rotate one eye at a time and can look in two different directions at once!

➤ A male can grow to be 27 in. (68.5 cm) long.

—Jim Murphy,
Herpetologist Emeritus,
Smithsonian Institution

19

"If I were a chameleon, seeing that strange cat over there would make me change to whatever color means scared," said Riley.

"And for a good reason," said Aunt Martha. "That's a fossa, not a cat. It is the island's largest predator and it can jump and climb trees."

"They hunt lemurs, including aye-ayes," said Uncle Max.

"Oh no," said Alice.

"But fossas aren't their biggest threat," said Uncle Max. "Lemurs are most threatened by humans and **invasive** species, animals that were brought here from other countries. Farmers cut and burn trees that are home to lemurs and other wildlife so they can plant crops and raise zebu cattle or other nonnative animals. Eventually, nothing grows. The ground washes away, so farmers must clear more of the forest."

Fossa

➤ It is a shy animal that prefers to be active at night.

➤ While it looks like a cat, there are no wild cats on Madagascar. The fossa is more closely related to the mongoose.

➤ It can climb trees, which helps it to catch lemurs.

—Dr. P. J. Stephenson, Coordinator, Africa & Madagascar Program, World Wildlife Fund

> It is the fourth-largest island in the world, about the same size as Oregon and California combined.

> The baobab tree is its national symbol.

> Eight out of every ten creatures in Madagascar exist nowhere else on earth.

> Ninety percent of the island's original vegetation has been cleared.

—Yvette Razafindrokoto, Research Scientist, Wildlife Conservation Society

Madagascar

Uncle Max chose their path that night. Riley wanted to hold his uncle's hand, but he didn't want anyone to know he was scared.

"Uncle Max, the lemurs we've seen look friendly and cuddly. What is so different about an aye-aye?" asked Riley.

"It's the size of a cat," said Carlos.

"With ears like a bat," said Aunt Martha.

"Plus a long, furry tail and sharp teeth like a squirrel," said Brigitte.

"And a long, bony finger like a skeleton!" said Alice, poking Riley with a stick.

Riley screamed, then turned bright red.

"That's it! I want to go home!"

23

Uncle Max put his
arm around Riley.
"Listen, Carrot Top.
Aye-ayes may be funny-
looking, but you have
nothing to fear. They
won't hurt you. Plus,
their round eyes glow
in the dark, like night-
lights in the forest."

"Thanks, Uncle Max," sighed Riley, smiling for the first time all night.

"It's okay to be scared," said Aunt Martha. "And you can talk to us about it anytime." They searched late into the night, but didn't see any aye-ayes.

After a couple hours of sleep, a noise woke Riley with a start. He pulled open the curtains—and saw two glowing lights! But this time, he wasn't scared. In fact, he knew just what to do. . . .

Riley woke the others, and they rushed outside for a better look.

"Is everything okay?" asked Jaona, running up the path.

"**Aye**," said Uncle Max. "Or should I say aye-aye?" Jaona froze.

"It is strange-looking, but really not that scary," said Riley. "Just think of it as a night-light!"

"I'll try," said Jaona.

Aye-Aye

➤ The aye-aye's sharp hearing helps it find grubs crawling in dead wood.

➤ Its long, bony middle finger lets it spear grubs and insects deep inside the wood and pull them out.

➤ It is not a picky eater, eating insects, nuts, eggs, and even honey.

—Steven Goodman,
Coordinator of the Ecology
Training Program, World Wildlife
Fund, Madagascar

The aye-aye scratched the tree limb using its finger,
pulled out a fat grub, and popped it into its mouth.
"Not exactly movie star behavior," said Aunt Martha.

Suddenly, the camera light came on and Carlos and Brigitte were right there, filming away.

Alice smiled. "I don't know, Mom, for this movie, I'd say the star was acting perfectly."

"What a great quote," said Carlos. "Can we use it in the film?"

"Of course!" said Alice, beaming.

"Thanks to Riley, our mission to capture an aye-aye on film was a success!" said Uncle Max. "What a great honor to find an animal that scientists once thought was extinct. Now we can show the world that there is hope for the aye-aye—and hope for Madagascar."

Back at school, Riley explained that while Madagascar had no lions or elephants, it had important animals that existed nowhere else and were in danger of becoming extinct. He told them all about the hissing cockroach, the leaf-tailed gecko's camouflage, and the aye-aye's moonlight munching.

He returned to living the life of a nine-year-old, until he got his next letter from Uncle Max.

Where will Riley go next?

Further Information

Glossary:

aye: another word for "yes"

continent: a large land mass, such as Africa, Antarctica, Asia, Australia, Europe, North America, and South America

endemic: something that is from a given area (not foreign)

headlamp: a light attached to a band that is worn around one's head

invasive: something that is not from a given area (foreign)

iris: the part of the eye that controls how much light is let in

kitoza: dried beef, usually served with rice porridge

nocturnal: to be awake and active mainly at night

pollinate: to move the fine dust produced in seed plants from the stamen to the pistil of the flower so that it can bloom

territory: the area that an animal considers its home

Newly Discovered!

Two new lemur species have been discovered in Madagascar! The first, *Microcebus lehilahytsara*, is the size of a mouse and was named after Steve Goodman (the scientist featured on page 28). *Lehilahytsara* is Malagasy for "good man." The second lemur, *Mirza zaza*, is the size of a squirrel and is dedicated to the children of Madagascar. *Zaza* is Malagasy for "child."

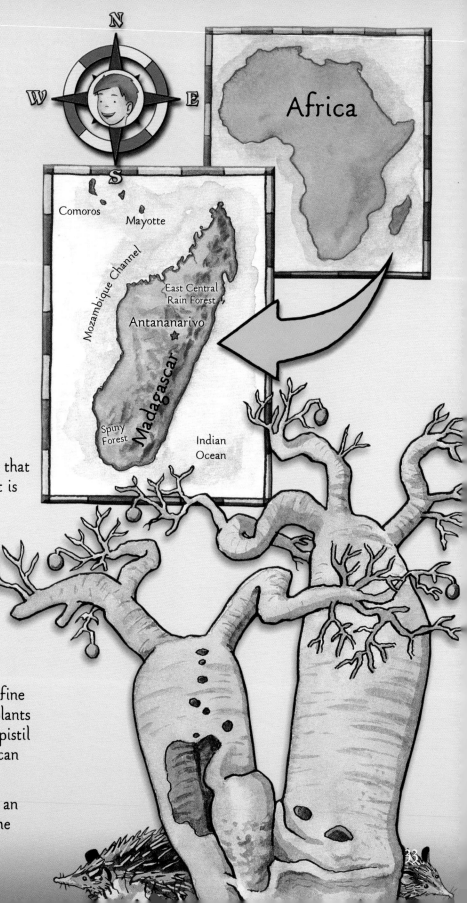

Africa

Comoros
Mayotte
Mozambique Channel
East Central Rain Forest
Antananarivo
Madagascar
Spiny Forest
Indian Ocean

JOIN US FOR MORE GREAT ADVENTURES!

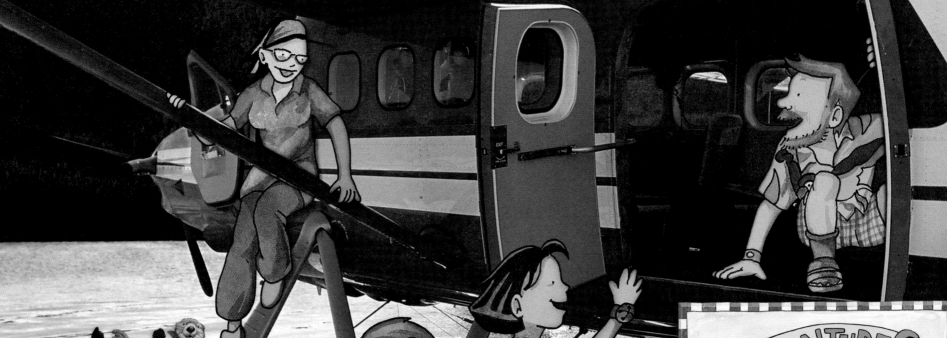

RILEY'S WORLD™

Visit our Web site at
www.adventuresofriley.com
to find out how
you can join Riley's
super kids' club!

ADVENTURES OF RILEY®

Look for these other
great Riley books:

➤ Operation Orangutan
➤ Survival of the Salmon
➤ Amazon River Rescue